A LINCC _. \JHIRE
RAILWAY CENTRE

A. J. LUDLAM

Published by the
Lincolnshire Wolds Railway Society

Louth-based class C12 4-4-2T No 67379 stands in the bay
platform at Louth with the morning passenger train for
Willoughby on 24th July 1952. No 67379 was a long-serving
Louth engine, built by the Great Northern Railway in 1901. It
served at Louth from 1925 until 1955 when it was moved to
New England from where it was condemned in 1958. *H. B. Oliver.*

MANCHESTER, SHEFFIELD, AND LINCOLNSHIRE AND EAST LINCOLNSHIRE RAILWAYS.

HULL TO LOUTH.

TIMES OF DEPARTURE ON AND AFTER THE 1ST OF MARCH, 1848.

Down Trains from Louth to Hull.

STATIONS.	1 1, 2, & 3 Parliamy.	2 1 & 2 Express.	3 1 & 2	4 1 & 2	5 1 & 2 Express.	Sunday Trains. 1 1, 2, & 3 Parliamy.	Sunday Trains. 2 1 & 2
	A. M.	A. M.	A. M.	P. M.	P. M.	A. M.	P. M.
Louth ....departure	6 0	8 30	11 15	4 0	5 30	9 0	5 0
Ludborough	6 11	... ...	11 26	... ...	5 41	9 11	5 11
North Thoresby	6 17	... ...	11 32	... ...	5 47	9 17	5 17
Holton le Clay	6 23	... ...	11 38	... ...	5 53	9 23	5 23
Waltham	6 29	... ...	11 44	... ...	5 59	9 29	5 29
Great Grimsby	6 39	8 57	11 54	4 27	6 9	9 39	5 39
Great Coates	6 45	... ...	12 0	... ...	6 15	9 45	5 45
Stallingborough	6 52	... ...	12 7	... ...	6 22	9 52	5 52
Habrough	7 1	... ...	12 16	... ...	6 31	10 1	6 1
Ulceby.................................	7 7	... ...	12 22	... ...	6 37	10 7	6 7
Goxhill	7 16	... ...	12 31	... ...	6 46	10 16	6 16
New Holland	7 20	9 28	12 35	4 58	6 50	10 20	6 20
Hull ....arrival about	8 0	10 0	1 15	5 30	7 15	11 0	7 0

In time for trains to Manchester, York, Leeds, &c.

Up Trains from Hull to Louth.

STATIONS.	1 1, 2, & 3 Parliamy.	2 1 & 2	3 1 & 2 Express.	4 1 & 2	5 1 & 2 Express.	Sunday Trains. 1 1, 2, & 3 Parliamy.	Sunday Trains. 2 1 & 2
Hull { Arrival of trains from Manchester, Sheffield, York, Leeds, &c.	A. M. 7 10	A. M. 9 50	P. M. 12 15	P. M. 2 45	P. M. 5 45	A. M.	P. M.
						10	
New Holland............................departure	8 0	11 0	1 15	3 45	7 0	9 0	5 0
Goxhill	8 7	11 7	... ...	3 52	... ...	9 7	5 7
Ulceby................................	8 16	11 16	... ...	4 1	... ...	9 16	5 16
Habrough	8 21	11 21	... ...	4 6	... ...	9 21	5 21
Stallingborough	8 30	11 30	... ...	4 14	... ...	9 30	5 30
Great Coates	8 37	11 37	... ...	4 21	... ...	9 37	5 37
Great Grimsby.......................	8 45	11 45	1 50	4 29	7 35	9 45	5 45
Waltham	8 53	11 53	... ...	4 37	... ...	9 53	5 53
Holton le Clay......................	8 59	11 59	... ...	4 43	... ...	9 59	5 59
North Thoresby......................	9 5	12 5	... ...	4 49	... ...	10 5	6 5
Ludborough..........................	9 11	12 11	... ...	4 55	... ...	10 11	6 11
Louth ....arrival	9 20	12 20	2 13	5 4	7 58	10 20	6 20

The STEAM PACKET leaves HULL *Half-an-hour* before the advertised Time of Departure of the Trains from New Holland.

Passengers are recommended to be at the Stations Five Minutes earlier than the time specified.

No Passenger can be re-booked by the same Train at any intermediate Station.

The Company will only hold themselves responsible for Luggage when it is booked and paid for according to its value; but they strongly recommend passengers to have their names and destination, in all cases, legibly marked thereon.—First and Second Class Passengers allowed 1 cwt. free of charge; Third Class Passengers allowed 64lbs.

Children under 3 years of age conveyed free, and those above 3 and under 12, conveyed at Half-Fare.

MANCHESTER, January 28, 1848.

BY ORDER.

ISBN 978-0-9926762-1-6

The Lincolnshire Wolds Railway Society would like to thank Alf Ludlam and Phil Eldridge for giving their time to compile this publication, and to Allinson Print & Supplies for their support with the project.

Printed by Allinson Print & Supplies, Allinson House, Lincoln Way, Fairfield Industrial Estate, Louth, Lincolnshire LN11 0LS

Issue 1. Spring 2014.

CONTENTS

Louth Class C12 4-4-2T No 67398 stands on the shed road at the south end of the station in April 1951. The engine retains its original tall dome and the title 'Louth' can be seen below the number on the buffer beam, as well as its "40C" shedplate on the smokebox door. *P. R. Batty*

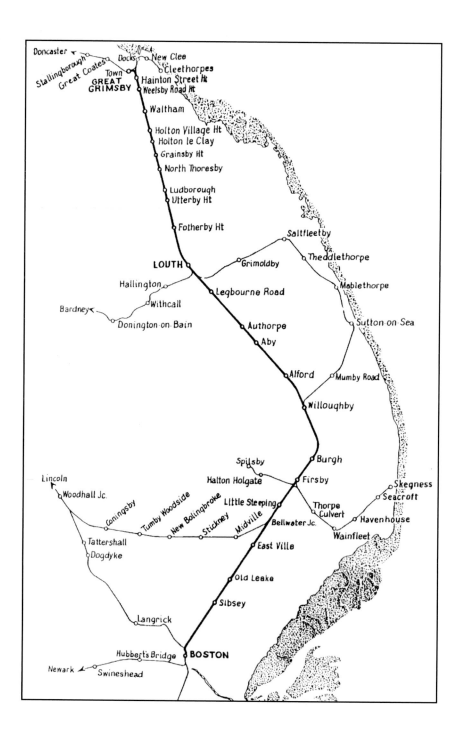

INTRODUCTION

The London and North Eastern Railway (LNER) "Holiday Handbook" said of Louth, "some of the most delightful scenery of the Wolds can be found in the neighbourhood of Louth, an old town occupying a picturesque site where the highlands merge with the wide levels of marshland, across which the lofty church spire of the town, 300 feet high, is a conspicuous landmark. Visitors to the Lincolnshire coastal resorts often make excursions to Louth, it is also a convenient  holiday centre for anyone exploring fen and wold. At the old Grammar School Lord Tennyson was a scholar for four years, and it was a Louth bookseller, Jackson by name, who printed the poet's first little book of verse, to which his brother, Charles, also contributed and was issued in 1827 under the title "Poems by Two Brothers".

In the 1840s Louth ranked next only to Boston and Lincoln as the most populous town in the old county of Lincolnshire, larger than Gainsborough, Grimsby, Grantham or Spalding.

A cheerful looking Louth station staff, accompanied by the stationmaster's dog, seen here during LNER days.

Constitutionally Louth was incorporated by Edward VI in 1551. A Warden and six Assistants of the town were appointed to govern both the town and the grammar school.

Louth owed its importance as a market town to its position at the meeting of the wold and fens. The principal chartered market was held every Wednesday, dealing with corn and cattle. The Saturday market dealt mainly with meat, vegetables, butter and fruit. From 1802 a sheep market was held every Friday during the Spring and Autumn and on alternate Fridays there was a fat stock market. Annual Fairs were held on 29th April for sheep, 30th April for cattle and horses and the Friday before 18th September, 28th October and 23rd November for cattle.

An attempt to bring the industrial revolution to the town saw the opening of a canal between Louth and Tetney Haven in 1770. However, the town was too remote for a future based on industry and the factories employed only a small proportion of the population, the majority earning their living in the outlying areas.

For many years Louth was a centre of railway operations in East Lincolnshire. It had motive power, engineering and signalling departments all based in the town. The railway was the largest employer in the district.

The Upper half of this Sheet is to be detached from the Warrant, and retained for the information of the Proprietor.

THE EAST LINCOLNSHIRE RAILWAY COMPANY.

(Incorporated by Act 9 and 10 Vict., cap. 88, 26th June, 1846.)

The within-mentioned DIVIDEND, Payable 15th OCTOBER, 1919, is issued by the GREAT NORTHERN Railway Company, *to the Proprietors of the East Lincolnshire Railway, on the Register of the Company on the 30th September, 1919, in respect of the Rent of Six per cent. per annum, guaranteed by the Great Northern Railway Company on the Capital of £600,000 of the East Lincolnshire Railway Company*—FOR THE SIX MONTHS ENDING THE 30th SEPTEMBER, 1919.

The following Statement shows the deductions made from the Dividend payable, viz. :—

SIX per cent. per annum on £100 Stock from 1st April, 1919, to 30th September, 1919, Six Months			£3 0 0
Less Income Tax, at 6s. in the £	£0 : 18 : 0		
and 1½d. per £25 Stock for Cost of Management for Six Months*	0 : 0 : 6		
			0 18 6
NET AMOUNT of Dividend on £100 Stock for Six Months			£2 1 6

* Authorised to be deducted by the General Meeting of the East Lincolnshire Railway Company, held 28th February, 1851.

Proprietors claiming exemption from Income Tax may obtain, on application to the undersigned, the necessary Certificate to recover the amount deducted.

COMPANY'S OFFICES, KING'S CROSS STATION, LONDON, N. 1.   E. H. BURROWS, SECRETARY.

Class D2 4--4-0 No 4321 with a passenger train which includes the Louth-Grimsby Quad-Art set at Louth in 1936. Built at Doncaster in June 1898 the first five engines of the class Nos 4321-5 kept the straight running plate up to withdrawal. No 4321 was a Boston-based engine in 1936 and was withdrawn in 1949.

The installation of Louth's new 50 ft turntable in 1938, it replaced the original 1876 40 ft table. The steam crane carrying out the work came from Peterborough.

The 9.05 am Cleethorpes-Kings Cross passenger train in the charge of Ivatt Large Atlantic, class C1 4-4-2 No 4408, takes water at the south end of the station while Louth engine, class D2 4-4-0 No 4397, stands in the bay platform with the 9.51 am for the Mablethorpe Loop. *H. C. Casserley*

An unusual vehicle supplies shelter for Louth's strawberry roan shunting horse who, with its shunter, awaits its next turn of duty. An interesting collection of freight wagons and tanks in the background and to the left posters advertising Conways Champion Beer, Andrews Liver Salts and Camp Coffee. When this photo was shown to Tom Eyre, a former linesman, his interest was in the telegraph pole, "Before we put it into the ground we drilled up from the bottom and then across to meet the hole above ground level. We plugged the bottom and dropped the pole into the hole. We used to pour old engine oil into the drilled hole, which preserved the pole for years".

Billy Bourne and a strawberry roan shunting at the north end of Louth station in July 1939. This photo taken by J. W. White of High Holme Road, Louth, and entered into the LNER Photographic Circle. It was voted best in the 'Iron Road' competition.

Horse shunter Jim Green, 'Dick', Stationmaster Hammond, horse shunter Billy Bourne and 'Tushy' outside Louth station on the occasion of the Coronation of King George VI in 1937.

An immaculate Ivatt Large Boilered Atlantic class C1 4-4-2 stands alongside the water column with a Cleethorpes-Kings Cross passenger train. The engine crew wait the right away signal from the guard.

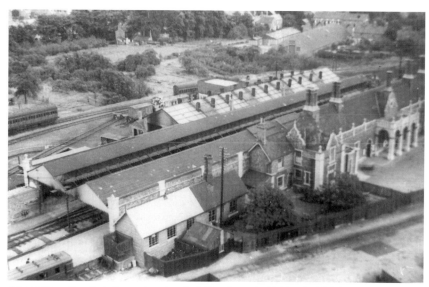

An overview of Louth station and engine shed taken from the Maltings in 1950. The elegant station building and stationmaster's house stand in front of the overall roof, engine shed and turntable. *H. L. Howe*

Two forms of transport, 'Dick' the station horse complete with horse brasses and driver stand alongside a lorry with a **LNER** removal container aboard. *H. L. Howe*

THE ARRIVAL OF THE RAILWAY

The East Lincolnshire Railway ran from Boston to Grimsby Town where it joined the Manchester Sheffield and Lincolnshire Railway (MS&LR) and on to New Holland and beyond.

The foundation stone for Louth station was laid on 8th July 1847, by Miss Charlotte Pye, the 16 year old daughter of Henry Pye, a Director of the ELR company. The architects were Weightman and Hadfield and the builder John Dales.

By October the centre section and side wings were built ready for roofing. Progress was being made on a large warehouse to the north of the station. The gatehouse at the crossing with Brakenborough Road was finished and being utilised as an office. By September the station roof was completed, a gasworks finished and ready to work, and piles were being driven for the foundation of the engine shed on the eastern face of the station building.

The completed station building was in a handsome Jacobean-style with curved red brick stone-capped gables, a balustraded roof with linked chimney stacks and a superb stone round-arched Porte-Cochère with Renaissance details. The platform side was unusually constructed of white bricks. An overall roof covered the platforms and running lines,

The approach and Jacobean-style station buildings seen at their best on 11th July, 1959, surely one of the most elegant buildings on the GNR system. The chap on the extreme right is contemplating a notice board advertising "Holiday Runabout Tickets". *H. B. Priestley*

9

supported between the rails by a series of elegant cast iron pillars.

A few years later a stationmaster's house was added, very much in sympathy with the main building. Other changes occurred over the following years, including the destruction of the original wooden goods shed during a fierce gale on 28th May 1860. This was replaced by a large brick building of typical Great Northern Railway (GNR) architectural style. Although the ELR remained independent until the 1923 grouping, it was operated by the GNR from the outset.

In January 1879 a temperance refreshment room was opened at the station by the Holy Trinity Temperance Association. This group and others were involved in a petition sent to Parliament protesting against the trade in "seduction and prostitution" brought about by the facilities for travel afforded by the railways and the resulting increase in female immorality. "Young females, 15 to 20 years old are watched on the approach of London trains and by lying and subtlety are led away to their ruin".

On Friday 17th September 1847, some of the ELR Directors and their friends travelled over the line to Grimsby. The train, comprising of two GNR carriages, left Keddington Road gatehouse at 2.02 pm, amid streaming flags and cheers from thousands of onlookers. The train returned at 5.30 pm welcomed by the ringing of the parish bells.

The Louth to Grimsby section opened officially on 1st March 1848, both GNR and MS&LR trains running between Louth and New Holland, where they connected with the Humber ferry.

By 3rd September the line had reached Firsby and the final section between there and Boston was completed by the end of September and the whole line opened on 2nd October 1848.

Six weekday trains were advertised between Boston and New Holland, with connections to London Bishopsgate Street or Euston Square. Three trains in each direction were provided on Sundays. First and second class market and day tickets were issued to Boston from stations on the ELR between Alford and Boston. By 1849 market trains for Boston were leaving Gainsborough and Louth at 7.10 am, calling at all intermediate stations and returning from Boston at 4.30 pm every Wednesday and Saturday. Louth regarded itself to be of equal importance to Boston and petitioned that it should be given equal privileges, particularly as its market day coincided with that of Boston.

The first engines to work over the ELR were Sharp Singles Nos 1 and 2, this photo shows No 1 rebuilt as a tank engine and seen here as running in 1864. *Kenneth Leech*

The Masons Arms Hotel horse-drawn omnibus which would collect visitors at Louth station and transfer them to the hotel.

Stirling's elegant main-line express 8ft 4-2-2 Singles were relocated to Lincolnshire at the end of their working lives. No 1003 is seen here at Boston on 14th April 1914, it was the last to be withdrawn the following year on 6th May. No 1008 was shedded at Louth from where it was withdrawn on 5th June 1914. *Kenneth Leech*

Class D3 4-4-0 No 4307 (left) outside the south end of Louth shed with No 3814, the last of the Stirling 2-4-0s alongside in 1927.

A Stirling class F 0-4-2 stands near the newly-opened Louth South signal box in 1887. This is a rare photo of the footbridge that once stood at the south end of the station. The signal box was built in conjunction with the construction of a bay platform to deal with branch line traffic to Mablethorpe and Bardney. The presence of the bridge restricted the signalman's view along the platform. It was demolished and replaced by a subway, which was unique in Lincolnshire.

206 series 2-4-0 No 1000 as rebuilt to class E1 in 1905 and fitted with an Ivatt-style cab. Shedded at Louth, and a well-liked engine and latterly kept going for only three turns a week, until withdrawn in January 1924. *Kenneth Leech*

13

The subway seen here in April 1970, the station's closure just months away.

Louth South signal box; one can see how the presence of a footbridge on the platform would have impeded the signalman's view. Note the water tank attached to the engine shed and the attractive station lamp on the right.

Class C12 67364 stands outside Louth shed. Classmate 67384 can be seen just inside the north end of the building. *N. Stead*

A container being off-loaded onto a railway road vehicle by Louth yard crane.

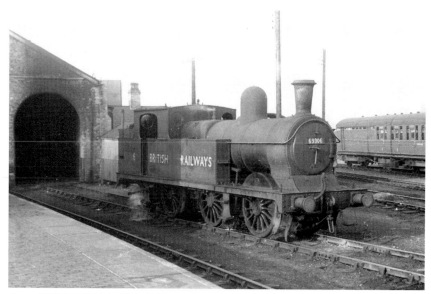

An ex-GCR class N5 0-6-2T No 69306 stands on the shed road at the south end of Louth station. Built for the MS&LR in May 1898, No 69306 arrived at Louth in 1938 and left in 1953, seen here on 27th October 1951. *N. Stead*

The north end of Louth engine shed on 15th May 1954, a class J11 0-6-0 stands on the turntable accompanied by class C12s No 67384 in the foreground and an unidentified class member in the shed. *B. Yale*

LOUTH ENGINE SHED

In the early days of the ELR Sharp Singles, converted to 2-2-2 tank engines at Boston works, worked semi-fast passenger trains over the line. By the 1860s "Small Hawthorn" 2-2-2 Singles were working trains between Boston and Grimsby, Nos 67 and 70 were still in Lincolnshire in 1890. Hawthorn 0-4-2 goods engines took over passenger services after 1890, No 101A worked the Mablethorpe branch in the charge of driver Cheeseman for many years.

"Large Hawthorn" 2-2-2 Singles were relegated to Lincolnshire as main line loadings increased and were used locally on secondary and stopping train duties in the 1880s.

Louth shed was host to some of Stirling's class E 2-4-0 passenger engines, which worked services to Grimsby, Mablethorpe and Willoughby. No 1000A spent its last days at Louth doing three turns a week. The last of the class, No 3814, was withdrawn from Louth in November 1927.

Stirling class F 0-4-2 tender engines handled mixed-traffic and were widespread in Lincolnshire until 1921. One of the last survivors, No 958, was shedded at Louth and sub-shedded at Mablethorpe.

One of Stirling's elegant main line 8ft Singles, No 1008, was at Louth from where it was condemned on 5th June 1914. Several of these engines finished their working lives on Lincolnshire lines.

After World War 2 Louth engine shed's allocation of engines was class D3 4-4-0 No 62132 built in 1896, two class J11 0-6-0s Nos 64320 and 64328 and seven class C12 4-4-2Ts, introduced in 1898, Nos 67352, 67364, 67379, 67381, 67383, 67384 and 67398. The D3 was taken to Doncaster for scrapping in 1951. The two J11s worked goods trains over the Bardney branch while the C12s were used on local passenger services to Bardney, Mablethorpe and Willoughby to the south and Grimsby to the north.

Through traffic at this time consisted of Immingham-based class B1s on Cleethorpes-Kings Cross passenger duties. Ex-War Departmental 2-8-0s and classes O1, O2 and O4 worked iron ore trains bound for Frodingham. Class K2 2-6-0 and J6 0-6-0s dealt with mixed-traffic goods from Boston to Grimsby and the powerful Gresley class K3 2-6-0s took the fast fish trains from Grimsby Docks to London.

Named class B1s included "Madoqua", "Dibtag", "Lord Burghley", "Fitzherbert Wright", "A. Harold Bibby", "Oliver Bury" and "Mayflower". The latter in pristine condition drew the train on the occasion of Brenda Fisher's return to Grimsby after becoming the first woman to swim the English Channel.

The class C12s were phased out in the late 1950s, replaced at Louth by equally-ancient class N5 0-6-2 tank engines, numbered, 69261, 69269, 69305, 69306, 69309, 69322 and 69327. Just prior to the closure of Louth shed in 1956 a number of larger tank engines, class A5 4-6-2, were loaned from Immingham, No 69812 being one of them.

By the end of steam the new Standard class 9F 2-10-0 goods engines and "Britannia" Pacifics were working through Louth, "Hereward the Wake", "Sir Christopher Wren" and "Clive of India" among them.

Diesel motive power began over the ELR with the arrival in July 1956, of the Derby lightweight units later replaced by the more powerful heavyweight units.

The Brush Type 2 diesels Nos 5500-19 were the first to be allocated to the London area, working there until late in their lives, at which point some of them turned up at Immingham. They were very much underpowered for dealing with the heavy fast Cleethorpes-Kings Cross trains and were eventually re-engined with 1,460 hp English Electric engines. Although an improvement they still lacked the necessary power for express workings. Much better were the English Electric 1,750 hp units, but it was the arrival of the Brush Sulzer 2,750 hp locomotives that answered all the problems of speed and power.

The south end of Louth shed on 10th June 1947. Class C12 No 7352 is on the shed road whilst a class N5 moves passenger stock in the yard. The shed originally had two through roads but by this time the one next to the station had been bricked up. *W. A. Camwell*

Louth engine class D3 2132 in the yard in March 1950. Although two years after nationalisation it still bears the LNER initials on its tender and number on the cab side. Built by the GNR in May 1898 she was condemned on December 1950. This engine was pulling a train which contained gas canisters which began exploding near Donington-on-Bain in 1946. The driver, Jack Ingamells, fireman Geoff Jackson and guard Arthur Dodman, were awarded the LNER Medal for their bravery by Sir Ronald Matthews, the LNER Chairman, at Kings Cross. *Mike Black*

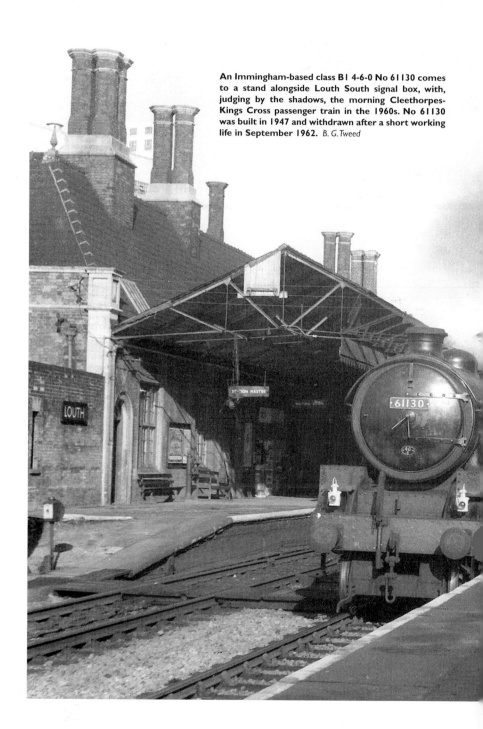

An Immingham-based class BI 4-6-0 No 61130 comes to a stand alongside Louth South signal box, with, judging by the shadows, the morning Cleethorpes-Kings Cross passenger train in the 1960s. No 61130 was built in 1947 and withdrawn after a short working life in September 1962. *B. G. Tweed*

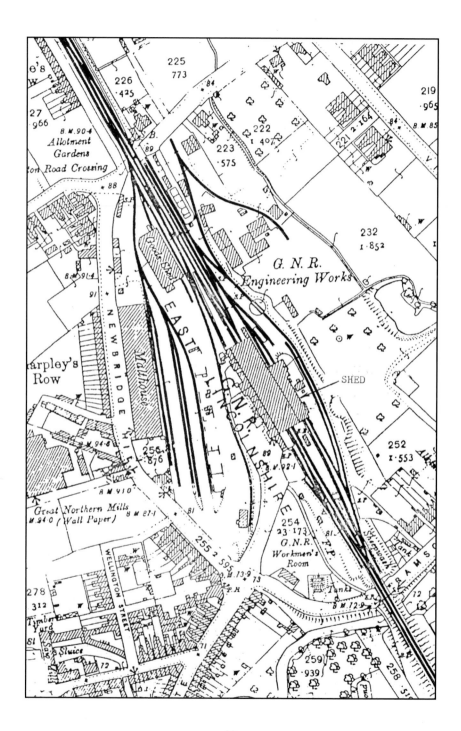

A busy scene at the south end of the station with class C12 No 67383 of Louth shed taking water and classmate No 67352 with a train for the Mablethorpe Loop. Note the contrasting bunker ends on the two locomotives. No. 67352 was one of the first ten of the class to be built, all of which had square corners to their bunkers and tanks, the rest of the class had rounded cornered bunkers and tanks.

The north end of the goods shed at Louth which replaced the wooden structure destroyed in a gale in May 1860. The sliced-off corner on the right of the building was made to accommodate the track running to the Maltings sidings.

Mablethorpe Junction was where the branch line to Mablethorpe left ELR. The signalman stands beside a fine set of somersault signals.

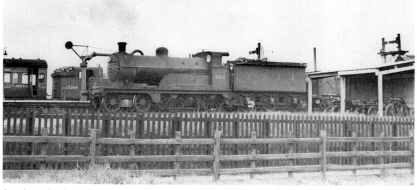

Louth station from the station approach on 16th May 1949. Class D2 4-4-0 No 2154 with a Boston-Grimsby goods train passes the bike shed and enters the station, while class C12 No 67364, with its bunker full to the brim, awaits departure with a train for the Mablethorpe Loop. Interestingly the C12 is in the new British Railways livery while the D2 still wears LNER livery a year after nationalisation. *P. H. Wells*

WORKING A TRAIN OVER THE ELR

Dick Dunnett was a young fireman based at Immingham towards the end of World War 2. He described a trip over the ELR. "We would book on duty at Grimsby Loco at the required time, have a look at the notice board and make our way to Grimsby Town station, where our engine would be waiting for us. Perhaps a "Lord Farringdon" four-cylindered engine with a load of 14 well-filled coaches.

We would take over from the Immingham crew who had worked the engine down from the depot. If they had done the job right they would have given the firebox a good plastering of coal and topped up the tender before leaving Immingham. I would check that the smokebox door was tightly closed, the front plate was clear of smokebox char as this could nearly blind you once
you got moving fast. Check that the headlamps were correctly placed and lit if required, that the water tank was full, the coal safely stacked and the fire irons racked. On the footplate I would examine the brick-arch to make sure it was complete, also that the gauge glasses were clean and functioning properly. Next give the firebox a good round to be burning through. Crack up as much coal as possible into fist-sized pieces, sweep and slack down the footplate and check the injectors. By now it would be time to watch for the guard's signal to move off.

The boiler would be three parts full and the steam pressure would be nearly lifting the safety valves. As we pulled round the very sharp curve towards Grimsby Goods signal box I would watch the passage of our train out of the station until it was on the straight and we were heading past Hainton Street signal box. I would now start firing going round the box with ten or twelve shovelfuls depending on what size of coal I'd managed to crack up earlier, slack coal was always directed into the back corners of the firebox. On with the exhaust injector as the boiler level would be now down to half a glass, the injector would be left on for most of the journey. Hopefully by now the safety valves would be simmering and the fire shaping into best steaming condition. The driver had no need to watch me, he could judge the effectiveness of my efforts by watching the smoke effects at the chimney which would tell him if he had the steam power required to work the train.

We would now be in sight of Waltham distant signal and if it showed clear another ten or twelve shovelfuls would go round the box and on with the other live steam injector as the engine was being worked very hard to get some speed into the train. From Waltham the Holton Bank was in our favour, allowing the driver to pull her up a couple of notches and we could now recover an inch or two of water. We would now be passing Holton-le-Clay and as soon as North Thoresby distant signal appeared another round of coal went into the box and on with the live steam injector. The slightly favourable gradient helped to gain the permitted line speed. A level stretch before the climb through Ludborough, off with the injector and another round of coal, this time a little heavier because of the gradient. Through the road bridge beyond Fotherby and the Louth distant signal would be right ahead. On with the injector, the line cleared left and then

(18) V 20—10,000—6-13. (W. & S. Ltd.)
Great Northern Railway.
TO
L O U T H

straightened out into the station. The train stopped at Louth; when the guard gave the right away off with the injector and watch the train out of the station. Fire up through the road bridge as the line was now bearing right through Mablethorpe Junction. Now a regular pattern of firing and feeding the boiler as we passed Aby and Authorpe. Alford station roof had been in sight some miles away; the approach was on a falling gradient. A pull up here to platform the rear coaches and then back to the old routine through Willoughby, Burgh-le-Marsh and on to Firsby.

From Firsby the line was level and dead straight until the approaches to Boston. Passing Little Steeping, Bellwater Junction, Eastville, Old Leake and Sibsey, most of these sections were of the same length and distant signals easily spotted. Firing was regular, to maintain steam pressure at maximum and water level in the boiler in the top of the gauge glass. The approach to Boston was over two very severe curves that were taken at 15 mph, first left and then right, then straight down the gradient to the water column at the south end of the platform. Off with the injectors while filling the tank, a quick flash around the box with the jet hard on to lessen the smoke emission and wait for the guard's right away.

Working days were conditioned by many factors, not least your driver and his handling of the engine. The reversing gear, if a screw gear, would usually mean he would use the steam provided by the fireman more economically, the reason being that it was not as hard to pull up on the rack and the expansive properties of high pressure could be used to best advantage. With a lever reverser - which often required considerable effort to notch up, the practice was often to pull it up to about 30% cut off and leave it there, not the most economical use of fuel and water.

The size and quality of the coal provided varied from huge lumps down to house fire sized nuts, slack and briquettes. Very few two days were the same, loads differed day to day, the same engine two days running could give you a good or a bad day. The shape of the firebed was important and required considerable skill to maintain it in best steaming condition particularly with some of the indifferent quality fuel provided."

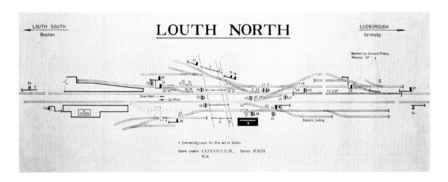

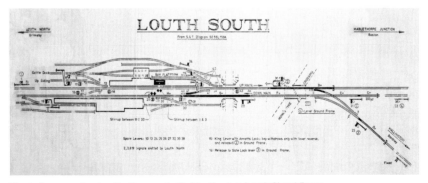

Track diagrams showing the lines controlled by the two Louth Signal Boxes.

The north end of the station with the goods shed on the left, the engineering department to the right and Keddington Road crossing and the line to Grimsby beyond. Class C12 No 4013, with driver Jack Ingamells and fireman Charlie Cox on board, has just taken water from the column on the platform. This was the column from which the crew of the class K3 were taking water when the German aircraft bombed the station in 1941. The cast iron sign on the right is headed "Up main cattle dock".

An Immingham-based class C4 4-4-2 No 62909 runs light engine in front of the cattle dock at the north end of the station. The goods shed is on the right and in the platform a class C12 awaits the right-away with a passenger train for Grimsby. *P. R. Batty*

Class D3 4-4-0 No 4314 stands at the south end of Louth station, its footplate crew standing next to Louth South signal box and in front of the bricked-up number two road of the engine shed on 3rd July 1936. No 4314 was a Louth engine from August 1931 until it was condemned in June 1937. Built by Ivatt for the GNR in 1898 it was one of a class of engines that were widely used on passenger traffic throughout Lincolnshire during LNER days. *H. C. Casserley*

STEAM RAILMOTORS

A motor train service operating between Louth and Grimsby was introduced on 11th December, 1905. It was worked by steam railcars comprising a small 0-4-0 tank engine attached to a saloon coach. The engines were in GNR green livery and the coach in the standard teak finish. The railcars were capable of being driven from either end and provided eight return trips daily.

Six units were built by, or for, the GNR and all of them at some time worked on the Louth-Grimsby and the Louth-Mablethorpe services. To accommodate the railmotor services halts were provided at Hainton Street and Weelsby Road, in Grimsby, as well as Holton Village, Grainsby, Utterby and Fotherby. These were basic facilities providing a short low platform for the use of the railmotors only. One such platform still exists at Ludborough station, the headquarters of the Lincolnshire Wolds Railway.

The GNR railmotors appear to have been the least successful of those built for various railway companies, due, in part, to their inability to pull a trailer car at times of heavy demand. This and their limited seating capacity were factors in the decision to withdraw them during the 1914-18 period.

GNR railmotor No 2 was shedded at Lincoln between 1912 and 1918. It worked out of Louth in the early days of the motor train services. Built at Doncaster Works in 1905, the coach section was the first to be built to a Gresley design, with a high elliptical roof which later became standard for all GNR corridor stock.

Class C12 No 67379 of Louth shed leaves Wragby station with a Louth-Bardney train on the last day of passenger services over the branch, 3rd November, 1951. The engine had been specially cleaned for the occasion and looks immaculate. *A. G. W. Garraway.*

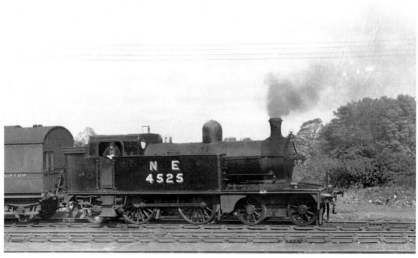

Long-serving Louth class C12 No 4525 wearing its abbreviated wartime livery, "NE" as opposed to "LNER" on 8th May 1946. *H. C. Casserley*

A powerful double-heading combination of an unidentified Ivatt 'large boilered' Atlantic and a class K3 2-6-0 with a passenger train at Louth in the severe winter of 1947.

The interior of Louth South signalbox.

Driver Jack Ingamells and Fireman Charlie Cook putting water into the tanks of Class C12 4-4-2T No 4013 at Louth station with the line to Grimsby and Louth North signalbox in the background.

Ex-GCR class A5 4-6-2T No 69810, of Boston shed, enters the north end of Louth station with an up class H freight train, with Louth North signal box in the distance, on 18th May, 1949. A late 1890s GNR brake composite coach and a NER carriage stand in the bay platform to the left. *P. H. Wells*

THE STATION BOMBED

On Wednesday 19th February, 1941 at 4.40 pm, a German aircraft circled over Louth station and dropped two bombs before machine-gunning the town. Both bombs exploded causing damage to the station buildings, rolling stock and some casualties, one of which, fireman C. Bradley, received fatal injuries.

The guard's room and store next door were practically demolished. The Goods Office, Porters' Room, Ladies Waiting Room, General Waiting Room, Booking Office, Lamp Room and Inspector's Office all suffered considerable damage, such as broken windows and fallen ceilings. The Stationmaster's house was badly damaged with broken windows, doors blown off and a large number of slates off the roof.

The engine shed received a direct hit which blew a large hole in the side wall of the station arcade. A Whitemoor-Frodingham goods train, with an Immingham class K3 2-6-0 in charge, was taking water at the station when the attack began. Bill Botham, the fireman, dived between the tender and the first van, which contained prams bound for Moisers in Grimsby. Percy Mouncey, the driver stayed close behind the water column. Both were lucky to survive when a bomb hit the platform near them and bounced into a dead-end siding before exploding. Bill noticed Percy clutching his face, his hands covered in blood. A piece of shrapnel had clipped the tip of his nose. The first-aid man at the station made a good job of sewing the loose flesh back in place so that, in later years, only a slight scar was visible.

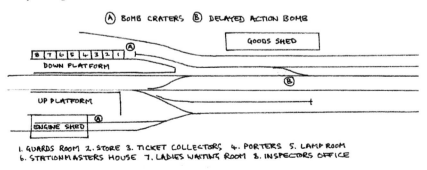

Ⓐ BOMB CRATERS Ⓑ DELAYED ACTION BOMB

1. GUARDS ROOM 2. STORE 3. TICKET COLLECTORS 4. PORTERS 5. LAMP ROOM
6. STATIONMASTERS HOUSE 7. LADIES WAITING ROOM 8. INSPECTORS OFFICE

AIR RAID AT LOUTH STATION

Some damage was done to the main line and it was assumed that a delayed action bomb was lodged there. This caused the down main line to be closed between Louth South and Louth North signal boxes. This arrangement lasted from 6.10 to 10.00pm, between which hours passengers were not taken past the affected area but goods and empty stock movements continued. A bus service between Louth and Ludborough was provided for passengers.

The site was visited by Mr Orchard of the Engineers' Department in Boston and it was decided no bomb was present. However, members of the Military Bomb Disposal Squad visited the site the next day and decided there was a bomb present and disabled it.

Louth station yard in the big freeze of 1947.

Coal merchants, including M. Jackson & Son Ltd, load sacks of coal in Louth Yard. *H. L. Howe*

A Railway Correspondence and Travel Society charter train at Louth on 16th May 1954. *N. Stead*

Goods vans occupy the line alongside the goods shed at Louth on 3rd October 1970. Keddington Road crossing and Louth North signalbox are seen in the distance.

Britannia Pacific No 70037 'Hereward the Wake', on shed at Immingham, alongside two unidentified class B1 4-6-0s in the 1960s. Initially the Brits worked passenger trains between Cleethorpes and Kings Cross and later fish trains. *Peter Clark*

CLOSURE

The Louth to Bardney branch line closed to passengers on 3rd November, 1951. Class C12 No 67379 took coaches borrowed from the Mablethorpe branch, Nos E88090, E86048 and E82861, on the final journey. The line was closed to goods traffic in sections, Louth to Donington-on-Bain on 17th September 1959, the section between Donington and Wragby on 1st December 1958 and finally the line from Wragby to Bardney on 1st February, 1960.

With the demise of the passenger service over the Bardney branch in 1951 several staff at Louth shed became redundant. These included three drivers, six firemen and six other grades including cleaners. The shed closed in December 1956 as a result of dieselisation. The last remaining steam engines, class J11 0-6-0 Nos 64320 and 64328 and C12 4-4-2T No 67398 were moved to Immingham.

The northern part of the Mablethorpe loop closed on 3rd December, 1960. The remaining section between Mablethorpe and Willoughby, on the ELR, closed on 5th October, 1970, a bad day for Lincolnshire railways after two public enquiries and a bitter battle against Dr Beeching's proposals.

The ELR closed between Firsby and Louth at the same time; the section between Louth and Grimsby remained open as a goods-only line, serving the Maltings at Louth. This arrangement lasted until final closure in 1980.

A railway preservation society had been formed which bought the trackbed between Waltham and Louth. The Lincolnshire Wolds Railway has established a base at Ludborough and reopened the section between there and North Thoresby. They are now concentrating on laying track to Louth.

Initially Louth station did not receive the kind of treatment such an architectural gem deserves. Suffering at the hands of vandals, an application to demolish it was made on 27th March 1987. This was thankfully rejected and it now stands, in modified form, as a testament to a time when one in five Ludensians worked for the railway.

Mike Pheby was Manager of the Travel Shop in Mercer Row, Louth, which opened in January 1966.

"Dr Beeching's proposal in 1963 to close the East Lincolnshire Railway meant that the nearest station to Louth would be Market Rasen, sixteen miles to the west.

Before the closure of Louth station, the Doncaster management of British Rail Eastern Division had considered this situation and contacting me requesting a visit from their Divisional Manager for a confidential meeting to discuss the possibility of our Travel Shop representing British Rail for information and ticket issuing.

Few travel agents at this time were also railway agents, so it was a prestigious appointment, and a considerable asset, to display the familiar red and white illuminated logo outside your shop in the High Street. The final decision to close Louth station had not yet been made, hence the sort of 'cloak and dagger' approach to our office.

We had already obtained agency recognition from airlines and passenger ship companies, so were well established in the developing travel trade and could be relied upon by the general public. This was further emphasised at the Divisional Manager's visit when it was made clear that when the station closed we would be asked to take over the role of the ticket office, but not to reveal this fact to anyone at present.

The Louth Station Ticket Office closed to the public on 5th October 1970 and the Travel Shop was duly appointed".

Louth-Grimsby coaching stock was, for many years, a quad-articulated set of **GNR** vintage, seen here on 16th May 1954 in the north bay platform at Louth station.

Wragby Junction where the Louth to Bardney branch left the **ELR. An ex-GCR class D9 4-4-0** passed the signalbox and crossing keeper's house with a southbound passenger train. *P. Grey*

Snow clearance near Louth in the very bad winter of 1947.

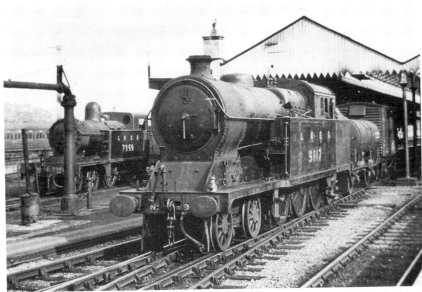

Class A5 4-6-2T No 9817 shunts a down pick-up goods at Louth on 18th May 1949. To the left is local resident class C12 4-4-2T No 7359. *P. H. Wells*

Coal being off-loaded from wagons into the coal drops in Louth yard at the north end of the station. Diesel shunting engine No. D2022 stands in the foreground.

Derby-built diesel railcars were originally built to work branch lines but were eventually used on services between Grimsby and Peterborough as well. Here on 8th January 1970 the 1.32pm departure for Peterborough waits close by Louth South signalbox. The overall roof no longer in place, a dusting of snow gives the station a seasonal look.

A desolate view of a once-proud station on 4th May 1975, when the track to Firsby had been lifted, the overall roof removed and the engine shed demolished. *D. Mundy*

Class 31 No 31113 has just delivered a vanfit of fibre glass to Associated British Maltsters at Louth on 25th April 1979, and approaches Keddington Road crossing on its return trip to Grimsby. The only surviving track from the Louth station complex are several straight lengths and the point and its lever, which led into the goods shed, seen here above, and just to the right of the white gatepost, which is now part of Pete Clark's private railway at Fulstow. *Malcolm Roughley*